MW00356395

CSS **Genre** Narrative

Essential Question
How are all living things connected?

Saving San Francisco Bay

by Yvonne Morrin

Chapter 1

Something Must Be Done!

In December 1960, Catherine "Kay" Kerr looked across Berkeley Bay from her living room window. Wind rippled the sparkling water as an osprey flew past. Near the shore, a heron plunged its beak into the mud, hunting for something to eat. Wildlife flourished in this part of San Francisco Bay (the Bay).

The view was certainly beautiful, but Kerr was frowning. Her friend Esther Gulick asked what was wrong. Kerr pointed across the bay to the land on the other side. There, the women could see bulldozers scraping up soil, sand, and rocks. They were pushing the material into the shallow water near the shore.

Many species of birds live in San Francisco Bay.

The bulldozers were filling in the shallow parts of the bay to make more land for the City of Berkeley. This was also happening in other parts of San Francisco Bay.

San Francisco Bay is an estuary. An estuary is a place where fresh water from streams and rivers flows into a harbor and mixes with salt water from the ocean. San Francisco Bay is home to many species of fish, birds, and mammals.

Kerr had read a newspaper article about plans to fill in almost all of the shallow parts of the estuary. She shared the newspaper article with her friend.

San Francisco Bay

Berkeley Bay

Berkeley

Oakland

San Francisco

San Francisco Bay

Pacific Ocean

San Francisco Bay is one of the world's largest estuaries, covering 1,600 square miles.

Many of San Francisco's smaller bays had already been filled to create more land. The two women realized that if the latest plans went ahead, the Bay would end up being just a deep river channel. Although ships would still be able to sail in and out, there would be no shallow areas left.

Kay Kerr and Esther Gulick wondered what would happen to all of the plants and animals living in and around the estuary. If the estuary were destroyed, some plants and animals could become extinct.

The women knew that pollution threatened the ecosystem of the Bay. **Toxins** from dozens of garbage dumps around the shoreline and even raw sewage were spilling into the Bay. Something needed to be done to protect the water, animals, and plants.

1849

1965

Berkeley Bay

2020

In 1849, San Francisco Bay was huge, but over time, many of its small bays were filled in. Plans to continue filling in the Bay would turn it into a river by 2020.

filled-in land

Kerr, Gulick, and their friend Sylvia McLaughlin set up a meeting with local **conservation** groups and presented their case. They urged the groups to help them. Everyone was very sympathetic. They were worried about the Bay, but they were already too busy with other projects to take on such a difficult cause. Kerr and her friends realized they would have to save the Bay and its animals themselves.

Wading birds, such as this blue heron, find their food in shallow water.

WILDLIFE IN SAN FRANCISCO BAY

San Francisco Bay is home to many different species of animals. Shellfish, snails, and crabs live in the mud in the shallow part of the estuary, and many types of fish swim in the water.

These animals provide food for wading and fishing birds, such as herons and egrets. They also provide food for the marine mammals living farther out in the Bay, such as sea lions.

Chapter 2

Speaking Out

In 1961, Kay Kerr and her friends set up the Save the San Francisco Bay Association (Save the Bay). Its goal was to prevent more of the Bay from being filled in. The women sent out hundreds of letters describing the damage caused to the Bay's ecosystem by filling in the estuary and asked people to help.

The response was unexpected. Ninety percent of the people who received a letter did not want more of the Bay to be filled in.

The women now had a lot of support, but they still did not know what could be done. Most of the land around the Bay was privately owned. It was spread across nine different counties. Each county's government could decide how to use the land it controlled around the Bay.

Esther Gulick, Sylvia McLaughlin, and Kay Kerr started Save the Bay.

The women had public support for their cause, but they kept being told, "You can't stop progress!" Saving the Bay seemed like a hopeless cause.

Then in 1962, the Berkeley City Council announced a new plan for more development. It involved filling in 2,000 acres of Berkeley Bay. If the plan went ahead, the size of the City of Berkeley would be doubled!

The women decided that stopping this plan would be their first goal. After all, Berkeley was their home city.

This refinery was built along the shores of San Francisco Bay in the 1960s.

WHY FILL IN THE BAY?

Developers and the city council wanted to fill in Berkeley Bay so they could use the extra land for apartments, parking lots, and shopping malls.

The new developments would provide jobs for construction workers, and the city would receive more money from property taxes. Cities around the Bay had to balance this issue of economic growth with maintaining open space.

The three friends knew they needed more people to speak out against the development of the Bay. They continued sending letters asking people to join their cause. They gave out bumper stickers to raise awareness so people would know what was happening.

By the end of 1962, Save the Bay had 2,500 members. They were all asked to write to the Berkeley City Council. Soon the council was flooded with letters opposing the plan.

The women also gathered evidence from engineers, city planners, and architects. They asked **ecologists** to explain what would happen to Berkeley Bay if it continued to be filled in.

The ecologists said filling in Berkeley Bay would cause an imbalance in the Bay's ecosystem. An ecosystem is a community of plants and animals that live together. All of the animals in an ecosystem rely on having other plants and animals available for food.

Aquatic plants and small animals such as mussels, clams, and crabs would die if Berkeley Bay were filled in. Then larger animals such as ducks, herons, and river otters would have nothing to eat. To save the animals and plants living in Berkeley Bay, the plan had to be stopped!

The women took this information to the Berkeley City Council. By the end of 1963, they had their first success. The council replaced the old plan with a new one. It greatly restricted how much of Berkeley Bay could be filled in.

Without the shallow waters of the Bay, river otters would have difficulty finding enough to eat.

Chapter 3

The Fight Continues

The fragile ecosystem of Berkeley Bay was now much safer. But what about the rest of San Francisco Bay? Its other small bays were still not protected from being developed. The women had won their first victory, but they knew their work was not finished.

In 1964, Kay Kerr met with a powerful state senator named Eugene McAteer. He listened to her with great interest. Then he set up a group to consider all of the plans for developing the Bay. The group met with people on both sides of this issue.

This cartoon uses symbolism to make a statement against filling in the Bay. What do the train driver, the man, and the woman represent in the fight to save the Bay?

"Curses—foiled again!"

Eugene McAteer helped Save the Bay in its fight to stop the Bay from being developed.

The group talked to developers who wanted to fill in parts of the Bay. They said it was important to do. It would create new land and new jobs. The group also met with ecologists, who explained why **preserving** the Bay was important for the environment.

Then journalists began to take an interest in the issue. A popular radio announcer named Don Sherwood joined the fight. He asked his listeners to write to their state legislators and urge them to save the Bay. The legislators were the people who represented them at the California state capitol in Sacramento. The legislators listened to them and suggested a new law. Any new proposals to fill in parts of San Francisco Bay would have to be approved by a state committee first.

Just before the law was passed in 1965, a permit
for a new project was approved. It allowed the top
of a mountain to be crumbled into soil and used
to fill in an area of the Bay. Then the space where
the mountain had been, and the new land created
by dumping it into shallow water, would be used for
housing. It would cover an area the size of Manhattan
in New York City. The new law was too late to stop
this development. This was a huge threat to the San
Francisco Bay ecosystem!

Kay Kerr (top), Sylvia McLaughlin (left), and Esther Gulick fought to protect the ecosystem of San Francisco Bay.

ENEMIES OF PROGRESS?

In the 1960s, many people didn't realize that human activity can damage the environment as much as can natural events, including droughts and earthquakes. The three women who established Save the Bay met strong resistance from developers who saw them as opposing economic progress.

Gradually, the public became aware of the impact of human activity on the environment. Books such as *Silent Spring*, published in 1962, discussed the effects of pollution. This book captured people's attention and helped start the environmental movement.

Save the Bay decided to sue the developers to try to stop the project. It was the first time an environmental organization had been allowed to represent the public in court. The court case dragged on for nine years, but Save the Bay didn't give up. Finally, the two sides reached an agreement. The project didn't proceed, and the estuary was preserved. It was a major victory for the environment.

Kay Kerr and the other members of Save the Bay were some of the first Americans to join forces to try to save the environment. They started a movement that showed how people working together can achieve big changes.

The organization is still running today. Its latest project is preventing plastic bags from polluting the Bay. The bags are dangerous because wildlife can become tangled up in them.

Like Kay Kerr and her friends, the members of Save the San Francisco Bay Association are still dedicated to protecting the environment. After all, people are part of the ecosystem, too!

Keeping trash out of the Bay is Save the Bay's latest project.

Respond to Reading

Summarize

Use important details from *Saving San Francisco Bay* to summarize the selection. Your graphic organizer may help you.

Main Idea
Detail
Detail
Detail

Text Evidence

1. What text features help you identify *Saving San Francisco Bay* as narrative nonfiction? GENRE

2. What is the main idea of the sidebar "Why Fill in the Bay?" on page 7? Use details from the text to support your answer. MAIN IDEA AND KEY DETAILS

3. What is the meaning of the word *issue* on page 10? Use sentence clues to help you figure it out. SENTENCE CLUES

4. Reread page 9. Use details from the text to write about the effects that filling in the Bay would have on the estuary's ecosystem. WRITE ABOUT READING

Compare Texts
Read about food webs and their importance in an ecosystem.

The Great Estuary Ecosystem

San Francisco Bay's estuary is home to many plants and animals. Many clams, mussels, and other sea animals live in the mud. Fish, birds, and mammals live in the water. Other birds and mammals live on the shore. Endangered animals live there too, such as a bird called the California Clapper rail.

All these living things depend on each other. They are part of a **food web**.

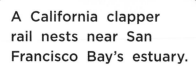

A California clapper rail nests near San Francisco Bay's estuary.

Seaweed and tiny water plants called phytoplankton grow in the shallow waters of the estuary. The plants need to grow in shallow water because the sun's energy can penetrate the water and reach plants. The plants use the energy to produce food. They are called **producers**.

Mussels, shrimp, and small fish eat these plants. The mussels are eaten by river otters, which also eat fish and shrimp. When animals eat plants, the energy from the plants is transferred to the animal. When animals are eaten by other animals, the energy is transferred again. Animals that eat, or consume, plants or other animals are called **consumers**.

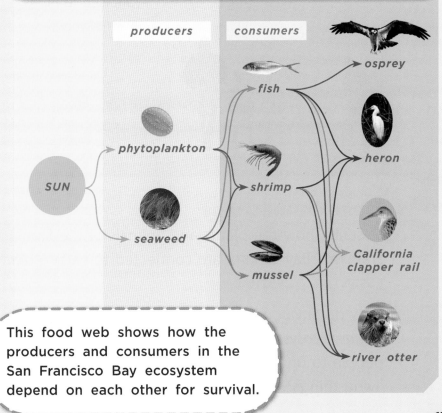

This food web shows how the producers and consumers in the San Francisco Bay ecosystem depend on each other for survival.

Some animals spend all their lives in the estuary. Other animals start life in the estuary where there is lots of food. They move into deeper water when they are older.

People are part of food webs, too. People catch fish and shellfish to eat in San Francisco Bay. If the Bay's ecosystem is harmed, there will be less food for people, as well as animals.

Children enjoy fishing near San Francisco Bay.

Make Connections

Describe how the plants and animals of the San Francisco Bay estuary are connected to each other. ESSENTIAL QUESTION

How do *Saving San Francisco Bay* and *The Great Estuary Ecosystem* show that it is important for people to understand the connections between living things? TEXT TO TEXT

Glossary

aquatic *(uh-KWAH-tik)* living in or near water *(page 9)*

conservation *(kon-sur-VAY-shuhn)* the protection, preservation and restoration of the natural environment *(page 5)*

consumers *(kuhn-SEW-murz)* animals that consume plants or other animals *(page 17)*

developers *(di-VEL-uh-purz)* people or companies that build and sell houses or other buildings on a piece of land *(page 7)*

ecologists *(ee-KOL-uh-jists)* people who study the relationship between living things and the place where those things live *(page 8)*

food web *(fewd web)* a system in which plants and animals are linked to each other as food sources *(page 16)*

preserving *(pri-ZURV-ing)* keeping something safe from harm *(page 11)*

producers *(pruh-DEW-surz)* plants that produce food for other animals *(page 17)*

toxins *(TOK-sinz)* poisonous substances *(page 4)*

Index

Focus on Science

Purpose To understand and describe how living things are connected to each other in a food web

Procedure

Step 1 Look at the food web diagram on page 17.

Step 2 Think of another ecosystem with different plants and animals that depend on each other to live.

Step 3 Draw a food web diagram that shows how the plants and animals in the ecosystem are connected.

Step 4 What might happen if one part of the web were changed or damaged?

Step 5 Discuss your diagram with a partner.

Conclusion What have you learned about how living things depend on each other? When one part of the web is changed or damaged, it affects the other parts of the web. What kinds of things can cause changes in a food web?